A DAY FOR LOVE

A DAY FOR LOVE

SHRISHAIL BHURKE

Made with ♥ on the Notion Press Platform
www.notionpress.com

I dedicate this book to someone special person in my life

Thinking a story for special person

about a very unusual friend

where you are the star of the my life story

from the start and right to the end of my life,

so dear enjoy this book

because it's written just for you!

and given with lots of special love

and lots of feeling which i cant express from mouth.

Contents

Contents

Acknowledgements

First and the foremost I thank to the Readers and my friendS for believing in me

And Thanking my parents for being suppotive in my endeavours

Thanks to our Dear Readers for picking this book A DAY FOR LOVE,

You're the beautiful part of our success,

Finally ,Heartfelt thanks to THE INK-O-SAPIENS-COMMUNITY OF PUBLICATION HOUSE AND FOUNDER SHRISHAIL BHURKE

"about The Author"

ABOUT THE AUTHOR SHRISHAIL BHURKE

Coruscating author Mr. Shrishail Bhurke is born on 11.03.2000, hailing from Humnabad, Bidar, Karnataka. He is an aspiring author who won numerous international and national records in the field of writing.

To him his parents, Mr. Shivraj Bhurke and Mrs. Bharti Bhurke are the finest supporters. Also he recently started his own publication name INK – O – SAPIENS, which is registered under government.

"ABOUT THE AUTHOR"

We know that, every writer is born with little inspiration and this inspiration comes from love and purity. Mr. Shrishail Bhurke always keeps himself lost in the thoughts of love so that he can present himself more beautifully.

He did his schooling in Ram and Raj Humnabad and his PUC in CBG Kardyal Bhalki in Karnataka.

Being as a writer, he has co-authored 50+ books and 10+ international books. Mr. Shrishail Bhurke won many numerous awards like, "India Star Republic Award" on 26th January 2021, as the best writer of the year, "Kalam International Golden Award" in Chennai at 21st February and on 75th Independence Day he got entitled with "INDIA STAR INDEPENDENT AWARD". Also apart from these awards, Mr. Shrishail Bhurke got featured on top international magazine, Mt. Kenya Times for his enhancing life, incredible talents in the month of February, 2021. Mr. Shrishail Bhurke also compiled a ravishing book named as, "Power Of Youth" and this book majorly got recorded by Indian Book Of Records. On Saturday 25th December 2021, he won INDIA PRIME AWARDS 2022 for being a finest entrepreneur of the this new decennium.

Moreover as a co-author, Mr. Shrishail Bhurke is candidly proud to be a part of the books which has hit several astonishing records like :

1) OMG Book of Records
2) Bravo International Book of World Records
3) Vajra Book of Records
4) International Talent Book of Record.
5) Insc. Award of 2021

From being a proper student to achieving numerous records and awards, Mr. Shrishail Bhurke staggeringly became a huge inspiration to many youth people in and around the writing field, public places also to this entire universe.

In the above passage as I mentioned, Mr. Shrishail Bhurke has compiled a book name called "Power Of Youth" which is highly dedicated to this society. And in that book, Mr. Shrishail Bhurke tells that, "Youth are burning embers, when kindled with quality education, right opportunities and passionate skills glows on a fire, that'll make the world more brighter and more beautiful someday."

According to Mr. Shrishail Bhurke's talent, we can admirably say that he's new generation Shakespeare and a commendable mentor of many authors like us.

The pulchritudinous part is, Mr. Shrishail Bhurke got featured on popular top magazine called "TAREE ZAMEEN PAR" where he received captivating medal, certificate of appreciation and along with that a written poem by him – "Will You Come Back?".

From biography of Mr. Shrishail Bhurke we can frankly learn a lesson, "In the end, we only regret the chances we didn't take. Hence, whenever opportunities knock your doorstep accept it on right away."

INK-O-SAPIENS-COMMUNITY PUBLICATION

"A DAY FOR LOVE"

BY;SHRISHAIL BHURKE

ISBN;

ENGLISH Anthology FIRST EDITION

BOOK Formatting;SHRISHAIL BURKE

COVER DESIGN;INK-O-SAPIENS-PUBLICATION

PRICE;

" A DAY FOR LOVE"

BY SHRISHAIL BHURKE

A COLLECTION OF THE FINEST POETRY

INK-O-SAPIENS-COMMUNITY OF PUBLICATION

Content

1. "ROSE DAY"

Red rose, the symbol of love
Which is eternal..
Hidden within the leaves..
Red blood in colour,
Everlasting coloured it has!!
That newly sprung in June
Dance with various tune..
God's beautiful creation
Rose and it's thorn
Made for each other!!
Gorgeous soft petals,
The perfume it holds
Quite alluring!!
Nobody knows that little rose
Bliss and everlasting beauty
And the divine never ends
Red rose ;child of mother nature!!

©shrishail bhurke

2. ROSE DAY

Roses are not red
When you are in bed

The day i presented you with a red rose,
That was the day my heart was fully exposed,

For that special rose to my love
Is to show how much I need you baby,

That special rose,
Will forever be to my heart close,

I will give you thousand of them, but that special one is the one I will use to seal our hands in strength

©shrishail bhurke

3. "ROSE DAY "

The enchanted hour,
The magic bower,
Where, crowned with roses,
Love love discloses.
'Kiss me, my lover;
Doubting is over,
Over is waiting;
Love lights our mating!'
'But roses wither,
Chill winds blow hither,
One thing all say, dear,
Love lives a day, dear!'
'Heed those old stories?
New glowing glories
Blot out those lies, love!
Look in my eyes, love!
'Ah, but the world knows -
Naught of the true rose;
Back the world slips, love!
Give me your lips, love!
'Even were their lies true,
Yet were you wise to

Swear, at Love's portal,

The god's immortal.'

©shrishail bhurke

4. "PRAPOSE DAY"

Hey my little star
Pretty like the maker
I accept your my lover
Little star till forever
I am grateful For you
I am happy for you
I believe in you
Baby I love you
You little eyes are my peace
You little voices are my assurance
You movements are my life
You breath calms me
Your little cry bothers me
You little tears,tears me too
You little smile is my light
You little hands are my home
How you say mummy,exites
How your exited to see me,
How you calm when I hold you
All of them make me feel blessed
My angel and my answered prayer
Friends know how much I wanted you

That warm sleep,keeps me staring
My pretty star has healed my scar
©shrishail bhurke

5. "PRAPOSE DAY"

My first crush
Though I tried to hide it....
I dare not say it out..
For the fear of religious battles...
I wish love will prevent the blood spills..
Just at the climate of the day sun..
The Muslim appeared..
No friend to accompany her..
Lone and exhausted..
Then a Christian saw the black beauty..
A perfect shade of hers..
Smiles and hope was seen on her face..
As they were locked in eye contact...
The beginning of friendship..
But in his heart.. She is more than just a friend..
She is just than irreplaceable friend
©shrishail bhurke

6. "PRAPOSE DAY"

I love you like I love the thrill of pure infatuation
But most of all I love you like a cherished friend
Who holds me tight, and loves me to the end
There is a face I'd love to see
Eyes I'd love to drown deep into
Lips I'd love to kiss.... YOURS.
When I kissed you, I was scared to hold you
When I hold you I was scared to love you
Now that I love you I'm scared to loose you..
You're my angel.
My lullaby.
Forever yours. Until I die.
You're my angel. My sweetest thought.
Eternally yours. My dear angel, the only one I've got.
I won't lie to you, for to lie to a goddess is a sin
I love your mind and soul
And I love you from heart to sheol
I can still smell your hair
I can still feel your touch
I can still taste your lips.
I can still see your smile.
I can still sense your closeness

And though at times a thread may break
A new one forms in its wake
To bind us closer and keep us strong
In a special world, where we belong.
The sharpness of your mind
The sweetness of your lips
The softness of your skin.
Your beautiful laugh
Your glorious smile, Your perfect body
An episode of passion, A night gone by.
No force could stop the attraction, Between you and I.
©shrishail bhurke

7. "CHOCOLATE DAY"

Let's talk about the sweetness of the brownie,
and the smile it bring to our lips ,
o lover, it's one way to see me smile
Let's celebrate
It's Chocolate Day
Yay sweets are tasty but chocolates are tastier
Time for your brownie
Let's celebrate your sweetness
perfect in all ramifications say yay it's Chocolate Day
you've brought smiles to the Adorable lips of kids
we will jubilate brownie ,
we will celebrate your day say Yay it's Chocolate Day
perfect day for your brownie
©shrishail bhurke

8. "CHOCOLATE DAY"

Being with u are like a chocolate
You can't survive on them single
Love is a like a chocolate
You should be enjoy with every bite of it.
Every chocolate is not taste
But from you are mouth it's different
Sugar is not candy
But your lips were tasty like a chocolate
©shrishail bhurke

9. "CHOCOLATE DAY"

Baby love you
Your lips were tastes like a chocolate,
Baby I wanna bite it and make you my soul mate!
Baby I wish you were chocolate to me,
That I liked you,
That I tested you, that baby I need you.
©shrishail bhurke

10. "TEDDY DAY"

My valentine ,My sweetheart.
The word is your's and mine,
Frozen together in a distant time .
I would run mile after mile,
To just see you and that gorgeous smile .
My valentine, My sweetheart.
My hearts is only for you,
Feeling like a dream come true.
You're like an angel from above,
And I present you with all my love
Baby I giving you gift
Don't left it
Baby happy Teddy day
©shrishail bhurke

11. "TEDDY DAY"

Hey small teddy
How do I kiss with you
Hey small teddy
How do i share my feelings without you
Hey small teddy
How can i dream without you
Hey small teddy
How can i live without you
Hey small teddy
How can i do sleep without you
Hey small teddy
Your like my love
©shrishail bhurke

12. "TEDDY DAY"

" THE TEDDY BUDDY"

Hey i can't ringing you today, baby.
I know baby You may be still sleeping tranquilly,
By hugging the mushy red teddy bear,
That I had gifted you just yesterday.
I know, you despise being left alone;
And always want an ally to cuddle with.
Though I can't be with you all day long,
Hope the teddy buddy will entertain you,
By thinking that I'm with you
You can hold it as much time you wish,
As the cute friend will never ever go away.
It will lend ears to your silly chit-chats,
Without exhibiting any sort of averseness.
We can also take it along in our outings,
And imagine it as our baby and pamper it.
The teddy buddy will remain as a token,
Of the stupendous fable of our courtship.
©shrishail bhurke

13. "PROMISE DAY"

LETS MAKE OUR PINKY PROMISE HERE!

Let's make a wish in front of the metro shower's!
We won't be apart from our beautiful journeys!
I don't believe I'm with you!
Lot of times, I dreamed of you in my magical world!
But I couldn't believe how I could make it true!
Now, we stand on the stage as the hero and heroine of our life platforms!
Angel's are come to give their blessing to us,
All are come to greeting us to live happily,
But my mind is lacking on something,
Let's make our pinky promise,
We won't be far apart from our minds!
Let's make a wish to live our lives happily forever!
©shrishail bhurke

14. "PROMISE DAY"

In his eyes,
I saw the stars
That made me forget my scars,
Walk on highways without cars
Holding hands singing like Bruno Mars,
Day by day, we drove each other crazy,
He kissed my eyes every morning and kept me busy
Like his daughter, he never allows me to be lazy
And tried to make my life look easy.
He promised me eternity,
The unending love full of energy
He took me to the moon through his story ability ,
And took me to places that were full of ecstasy.
©shrishail bhurke

15. "PROMISE DAY"

Rub. Rub. I can't tell you
You have to feel yourself
Baby, what's love?
I am talking about your eyes
What you have done
I've done myself
I can tell you things like
I love you...... Yeah
I ain't talking to you
Jump. Jump. Throw your feet
Well then you have a pair
Baby, i'm talking to you
What I have done
You have done yourself
Are you alright? Yeah
I can do things like
Take you in my arms
Baby, I promise u I will love u
©shrishail bhurke

16. "HUG DAY"

I NEED YOUR HUG

I need your hug
Hold my hands together and lock with your fingers .....
Hug me tight as tight as pillow ...
So that all my fears go away, and I can smell your romance ..
Look deep into my eyes..
So that I can see the colourful butterflies in your eyes ..
Stay close to my heart ..
So that ,my thoughts travel with in your heart ..
kiss at my forehead ,and stay for minutes ,hours and a whole day;
Baby I need your hug.
©shrishail bhurke

17. " HUG DAY"

Like the moon beams kissing at the sea ...
Let cool breeze ruffle over my smooth silky hair ,
And let it trickle you..
Let the God bless us by showering rain ..
Make my heart sing out loud..
I see the love when I look at your eyes..
Let it melt into memory and plain into songs ...
Everyday with you gives me a thrill ..
There is a place in my heart for you..
I can't explain the way I feel about you..
You are softness melt my heart ..
you are my song in every silence...
I need your hug in every pain I need you baby and I need your hug
©shrishail bhurke

18. ;HUGDAY"

Baby love me
Hug me,
Baby love me
But don"t dare to leave me
Because we have hearts
Deeper than the oceans Full of emotion
Hugs because we let them
Mix and mingle
And form new waves
Baby hug me it's lovely to
©shrishail bhurke

19. "KISS DAY"

"THE KISS POEM"

Your kiss, is the poem;
Being an avid reader, I yearn.
Let your love spells embrace me,
And blow out my ember within.
Curious I am,
You, an open book.
Let this tiny star whoosh our
Your magical cosmos within.
I'm on cloud nine,
Would love to bid a kiss fine.
Let you not mistake it with list,
It's just to kiss your tears goodbye.?
©shrishail bhurke

20. "KISS DAY"

Have i told you yet....
how muchyou mean to me
Have i told you yet....
How lucky I am to have you?
Have i told you yet....
How always you're my source of joy and the happiness you bring to my sorrowful world..
Have i told you yet....
That you the best thing that has ever happened to me?
Have i told you yet....
That I love you ....always have and always will?
Well in case I haven't ....
I want you to know that , you really are a sent angel from the heavens.
And that I mean all the words said in this text .
I LOVE YOU
to the moon and back
My queen as I am your king .
Kisses my love
©shrishail bhurke

21. 'KISS DAY"

Dear if kisses were rain drops,
Then I could send you showers,
If love was a person,
Then I could send you me.
Dear when you see the sun shining,
Then that's me smiling to you,
When you see the birds chirping,
Then that's me signing softly into your ears.
But dear when the clouds releases few drops,
Then those are my tears for I miss you,
When you feel the wind blowing,
Then that's my whisper to you of I love you.
Dear I miss everything in you,
From your smell to your tender care,
I always feel empty without you,
That's why I close my eyes each time to bring you close.
The love that we share,
Is neither like the morning dew,
Nor the sun rising from the east and setting in the west
It is eternal my love.
Dear if you could know,
That missing you makes my heart to ache,

Then you would never leave me alone,
And go away from me.
Dear my eyes are hurting,
Because I can't see you,
My hands are empty,
Because I can't hold you.
Dear if you could know,
That my lips are cold,
Because I can't kiss you,
Then you could come close to me.
Dear remembering you,
Makes my heart to cry,
But loving you,
Is what I cherish.
©shrishail bhurke

22. "VALENTINE'S DAY"

My love
My darling
How wonderful it is
To have in my life my queen
I want to hold on to you forever
And if forever doesn't exist Then until whenever
Because you're it for Mr
You are beautiful as the flowers
Even more than the roses
Because your eyes shines akin to the sun
Baby I love u lots
©shrishail bhurke

23. "VALENTINE"S DAY"

My love
If the sky is the limit
Then how did I find an angel like you my darling?
To you I will profess my feelings each day
Without fear or shame my love
You're like a galaxy of beauty
An ocean filled with love
And the one I would always want
I love you my darling
It's only been a while
Since we were in each other's embrace
And I still can't shake the feeling
That I want to be with you my baby
And I still can't get enough of you
I love u baby forever
©shrishail bhurke

24. "VALENTINE'S DAY"

Hey babe
I came to understand,
On this planet on many paths we pass,
I don't regret the path I took,
The path that made us met,
The path that brought my favourite icon my way,
The path that made me start a new life...
A shitty history we have,
Exes we made,
Heartbreak encounter we had,
Wetting our pillows we did,
Regretting having them we did,
But despite all...
Moving on we had to.
You are my star
My favourite icon babe,
Just the other day was your birthday it was,
The other day it was Valentine...
I never made you feel my presence but I won't apologize....due to
to the following reasons.

I dint celebrate because...
Making you special just a day,
That has never been my goal
You are special from the moment the sun sets till when can count the stars in the night...
I wanna treat you right
Make each day special,
My jealousy can't allow me que with all your friends tell you hbd or hpy valentines.....
Am sorry but I wanna be there when they ain't around,
When you need this guy the most...

Too bad to this distance,
Killing and torturing us,
Lonely nights,
Long calls to cover up ,
Chats to keep us moving ,
Am trying to kill the distance to have the chance to.. Just be there and give you my time and full attention babe.
I won't promise you earth but my love,
Promising you fancy dates and gifts I can't but my time,
But if we get a chance I will let you feel the vibe
Spending on you I can't hesitate,
Because with all on this planet with a sick heart its vague....I wanna feel you
Am waiting for the day I will be by your side all time.

Hey
Mrs classified whenever you are ....
I will come for you ,i will be coming soon baby
©shrishail bhurke

INK-O-SAPIENS-PUBLISHING

INDIA'S MOST AUTHOR FRIENDLY PUBLISHING HOUSE

Stay updated about latest anthologies, events etc.........

THANKS FOR READING OUR BOOKS

AND CONNECTING WITH US

9 798889 599289

Printed by Libri Plureos GmbH in Hamburg, Germany